City of Poetry

To Logan City

City
of
Poetry

Star Coulbrooke

Copyright © Helicon West Press
Printed in the United States

Author: Star Coulbrooke
Cover Art: Jane Catlin
Book Design and Layout: Robb Kunz

ISBN: 978-09977444-3-9
First Edition

Table of Contents

I
City of Poetry..9
Poem for the Neighborhoods of Logan......................11
Two Sides of the Road: A Walking Tour....................13
Sesquicentennial, City of Poetry..................................14
Iris on the Hill...20
Sandhills: Four Lessons..21
Yellow Yarrow...24
Poetry in the Dark..25

II
All the Butterfly Myths are True................................27
Ogden City Walkabout..30
Grove and Lake...31
Driving to Pocatello..34
At Eighty-Two...38
Buddhist Poet Meditates on Water............................39
Ute Ladies' Tresses in Wetland Pasture.....................40
Poem for the One and Only Dean John Allen..........42
Christmas Bird Count..45
Breath, a City Art Cento..48

III
Fry Street February..52
Of Balance and Grace: The Public Face of Leadership............55
The Gods...58

Lament of an Aging Bookworm...60
Love Song for Stan LeRoy Albrecht..61
In the Half Light..64
Karen..65
Wisdom from the Edge of Alzheimer's......................................67

IV

Facing Fears...70
Me Too..72
Saying It...73
The Witches Dance...74
Amanda, Among the Bones..76
What Ben Said..78
First Dance...82
Letter to a Friend...85

V

Seasons in the City of Poetry...87
Seasons in the City, Wild Wise Nature.....................................92
Poem for Who We Are...95
Love Poem for Logan City...99

Acknowledgments...103

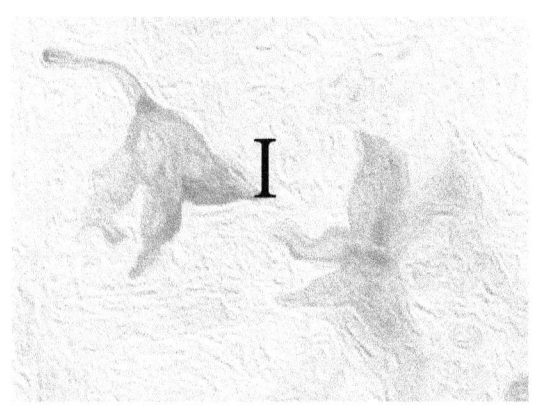

I

CITY OF POETRY

In Downtown Logan, where artists inhabit
bicycle shops and cafes, tattoo parlors and churches,
where paintings and sculptures and photographs adorn
the sporting goods stores and the old hotels,
line the walls along stairways and narrow aisles
among the coat hangers, above the tables,
along the counters near the checkout stand,
there's a bookstore mentality held-over from the days
when poetry was valued as artwork, as an escape
from the mundane workaday life, when people
would read it everywhere they went, memorize
their favorite verses, recite them over dinner.

Let's keep going there, keep going back to poetry,
forward to more poetry. Let's plaster it on the walls
of the City, compose our lines and stamp them
in cement at every new roundabout, every sidewalk.
Let's write poems to each other about our lives
in the City of Poetry where everyone, no matter who
they are, no matter what age or persuasion, what
family, what job, what form of transportation or
what inclination, will have a say, will know they matter.

Let's let poetry matter, let metaphor replace all
diatribes, all misunderstandings. Let's say it in poetry,
straight from the soul, not from media-feeds, not
from Google or TV or mass email, but out of the heart
where our stories reside, where our memories
and hopes don't fight with each other, where art
for art's sake becomes our priority.

Here in the City of Poetry, let's look to the backyards,
where families come out on a Sunday evening
to watch urban owls rise from blue spruce and juniper,
on silent wings, to go beyond the town and return
before Monday's first white dawning, swept with canyon
air from the forest's scent of summer to the paved
wide streets where our cars and buses take us
to work and to school, where we can think all day
of the stories we'll tell when poetry rolls off our tongues
like water over a spillway, fresh and clear and powerful.

Composed and presented for the Inaugural Ceremony
of Logan City Poet Laureate, May 19, 2015,
in the City Council Chambers, 290 N 100 W, Logan.

POEM FOR THE NEIGHBORHOODS OF LOGAN

For those who've been here
decade upon decade,
stately porches resting
in the afterglow of time,
children selling lemonade
out front, like their great
grandparents' parents
might have done before the streets
were paved, the sidewalks laid.

For those who rose up
in the fifties when the war
had ended, brick three-bedroom
houses neat and tiny, where
college kids and newly-marrieds
cozy-up behind back fences
for communal barbeques.

For those in subdivisions,
cul-de-sacs, with televisions
pulsing through front windows,
kids outside playing hide and seek,
parents with their feet up after
company, dishes waiting in the sink.

For those tucked in along the river,
wooden clapboard sidling-up
to rock and plaster, mansions
and bungalows sharing the fenceline,
willow branches dipping down

like curtains in the evening breeze,
a neighborly democracy.
For those within the cityscape,
for those on hilltops, those
of townhouses and seniors-only,
those of row-on-row apartments,
may they all endure as Logan
grows, as people gather, may they
pull together lightly, graceful
in their history, and ours.

Composed for the Logan City council
meeting on the topic of Neighborhood
Revitalization August 4, 2015.

TWO SIDES OF THE ROAD: A WALKING TOUR

On the hillside to our left, evening primrose
blooms ghost-white among short milkweed,
spike-leaved, clustered with tight yellow buds.

On our right, a golden deer. It claims the yard
where this house once made-up the neighborhood,
no others but the deer, four more appearing
among swing-set, playhouse, dark green lawn,
ears twitching, grazing as we walk on by.

Look left again above our newfound primrose
to houses hunkering like giants, plaster facades
grinning down the gravel delta, wooden stakes
and orange ribbons marking subdivisions
yet to join them, families with children waiting.

See the deer? They cross this road twice
every day, new obstacles to jump with every phase
of moon we'll soon see rising on the right
like half a lemon in the sky, salted with profiles
of backhoes, dump trucks, mortgage-makers.

Take heart for the swallows that dip and tumble
through the bug-thick dusk, gorging on mosquitoes
that whine past our ears as we swat at them,
as the peach-pink sunset spans both sides of the sky
and closes to steel gray clouds, yellow half-moon
haloing the grazing deer, burnishing the primrose.
And you, seeing both sides from the middle.

Revised from a previous version and presented for the Logan City council meeting on the topic of Neighborhood Revitalization, August 4, 2015.

SESQUICENTENNIAL, CITY OF POETRY
--For Logan City, Utah

I

Out of the wide open dirt roads
hard-packed for horse-drawn wagons,
out of the Telluride power poles
centered and towering next to the Eccles
trolley tracks laid down flat and gleaming,
out of the brick and wood buildings
rising shoulder to shoulder, archways
and awnings and signs painted-on,
Hotel Eagle, Cardon Jewelry, Temple
Grocery;

Out of the dirt road center of town,
not even a sidewalk to stand on, where
crowds gathered along the parade route
up Center and down Main, crepe paper floats
from the Rotary Club, Holstein Breeders,
Thatcher Clothing, and LK Wood of Mendon
with his miniature steam engine; out of
the Midwest to Logan, Ringling Brothers
Circus Parade, tigers and bears in cages,
camels draped in fine regalia with riders
perched high on their humps, showhorses
lined up single file, stately, a landscape
of mystery;

Down from the canyons, granite and lumber
for temple and theater, stone homes

and tabernacles, quarries where cliffwalls
were broken to blocks and carried to town
for lasting foundations; from brickyards
and lime kilns for plaster and mortar, for carbide
and water applied to make gas for the lighting
of businesses, banks, for the elegant homes
of the Thatchers and Nibleys, of the Eccles
and Youngs;

Down from tower of Old Main Hill,
down from the Victory Garden, Animal Science,
Dairy Science, Dormitory, down from Industrial
Mechanics, glass-roofed Conservatory, down
through Arts and Athletics, the Girls' Rifle Team,
gym class, junior prom, football, basketball,
Military Band, Second Platoon Company B,
down from the Red Cross Life Saving Corps,
five college women in bathing suits, red cross
centered inside a bulls-eye stitched to their
bodice fronts;

Out of the saw mills and grist mills,
shingle mills, water wheels, pick and shovel-
built canals and irrigation ditches, down from
Logan Canyon a drinking water system
named for the great Logan poet Aaron DeWitt,
a spring where water was so fresh and cold
pre-1940's, so they say, a person could
hardly drink it;

Out of the Model T's of the nineteen-teens
to the Bus Lines of the twenties, into the paved
stoplight sheen of gas and electric, plastic

and fiberglass, passenger cars in train formation
gliding the highways down to the valley
and into the City, a flood of endless residents,
of generations born here, leaving, then returning
out of the same nostalgia, out of the longing
for home.

II

What happened to all those places we knew,
those people who knew them before? ZCMI
into Howells then Wickels' then Mac's, then
the Kater Shop. Kater Shop's gone to the mall.

Knitting factories, garment companies,
specialty shops for ladies. Mode O' Day,
Keith O'Brien from Shamhart Christiansen.
Piggly-Wiggly, Woolworth's, Low Cost Drug.

Second Ward United Order Manufacturing.
The American Food Store's Saturday Special:
Two loaves of bread ten cents, hamburger
nine cents a pound, nine cents a dozen for eggs.

JR Edwards 1891 Saloon, the Club Saloon,
The Beach and Barracloch, Barracloch and Hansen,
Fjeldsted-Owens, Old Bitters, Boyle Billiards.
The Tap Room. The DelMar. The Cactus Club.

What happened to the drive-in movies,
one on each end of town way out beyond
the Main Street drag where stars encrusted

dark night skies above the lighted screens,
movie stars projected large and luminous,
cars of the decades parked in gravel, windows
rolled down for the speakers and heaters,
short walk to the restrooms, the popcorn stand.
What happened to Dragging Main,
cars full of teenagers cruising the strip
from Logan Lanes down to the Y,
from Blake's Spudnut to Pete's Spudnut
and back again, landmarks barely visible
to the few who knew where they were.

III

All along the corridor from Fourteenth North
to Logan River Golf Course, city of transition,
city of motion, city of welcome set down
in the center of one gorgeous valley
from mountain to mountain to mountain.

What happened here is what happens
everywhere, every year, in houses
built on every street, in apartments
nestled together like dominoes, in cars
that roll along from west fields to low
foothills, to what was once swampland,
frogs to be caught, bulrushes to break
into fluff and let go. What happened
was children, born to those who used to be
children too, here in this city that grew
like the bones of a growing boy.

Held in the bones of the city, people
of every persuasion who gather at churches,
at theaters, restaurants, people connecting
in friendship at school, at work, on the bus,
in libraries, animal shelters, parks, Rec Center,
zoo—those who say *We never want to leave.*
What happens is people, the best kind,
someone for everyone, a century and a half
of human history here in this city.

IV

It comes down to this: When your dogs bark
on a wintery Sunday morning, you look out
your window and there in the driveway,
two neighbors are shoveling your snow.
It's twenty degrees, yet you open the door
to smiles as warm as the full golden sun.

Or it comes down to this: The shuttle
from the car repair shop arrives and the man
who was already in the front seat gets out,
holds the door open, urges with the sweep
of his hand for you to take his place,
and when you arrive at the shop, he opens
every door, as if you were a celebrity.

Or this: The group of citizens who lifted
the crashed car from the motorcyclist's
broken body, pulled him free, made sure
of his recovery.

Or this: The dozens who
stood by our Muslim friends, citizens
whose lives became precarious when fearful
voices threatened to tear loose our solidarity.
Not one word of counter-protest for this
act of kindness.
This, our city, the one we've grown up with,
the one we claim, the one we hope will be here
to sustain us for as long as we are part of it,
part of what changes, part of what we hope
will never change: the spirit of community,
of history, centerpiece of our heritage, heart
of the valley, city of art, city of poetry.

Composed Jan. 17, 2016, for the Jan. 19, 2016 Logan City council meeting opening ceremony.

IRIS ON THE HILL

Every year they rise
from gray-spotted wilt
of last fall's dieback,
first green spears
piercing through muck
where deer punch narrow trails
down from maple hollows.

By early May, leaf-swords
press out in bunches,
swollen at the tips, shape
of deer-hooves or the folded wings
of birds. Iris on the hillside,
where peacocks fan their iridescent
tails at peahens ready to nest.

On the hill, iris of all colors
march down grassy slopes,
waving their flags
in the late spring breeze.

Composed as a longer version for the Logan Iris Society May 8, 2015; revised and published on a visitors' plaque at Red Butte Garden, Salt Lake City, Utah 2016; published in *Thin Spines of Memory*, Helicon West Press, 2017.

SANDHILLS: 4 LESSONS

I

Been down to the farwest fields
of Logan, searching for Sandhills
all afternoon.

Where ARE those birds?
I need to call Jack Green.
I need to find those cranes.

Been driving, not walking,
taking the long view,
the meadow view, grass view—

But 600 South going west
is the highway to Mendon
and traffic's impatient.

No one wants to wait
for a poet going slow, looking
for birds. They want to go home.

They want to get out in their yards,
push the kids on their swing sets,
grill a few burgers.

II

Those birds are elusive when nesting
in grasses, won't show themselves
to passersby on highways.

You have to get out and walk
like my sister and I did on a years-ago
June, up Cottonwood in Idaho.

Down a green hollow came bobbing
a Charlie Brown head, strange creature
we'd never encountered before.

Gawky and gangling, it toddled along
on thin legs through the Jacob's Ladder,
its body a gray-brown stem.

We stood transfixed until the pair
of red-capped parents hustled swiftly
downstream, long legs lifting.

Instant recognition. We high-tailed it
out of there, no legendary kick and thrust
required to save their chick from us.

III

My daughter lived across the lane from sand-crane
fields in Young Ward,
watched them from her front room window.

Leaping, bowing—head-pump,
food toss—she watched every feat
the sandhills use to pair-off.

For three years chicks appeared and grew
and lifted-off, then she did too, but unlike cranes,
her mate was not for life. She left alone.

IV

On the Platte River, Sandhills, Greater
and Lesser. Four feet tall, wingspan seven.
Weight, twelve pounds. Lifespan twenty.

Lesson 1: What of life's accomplishments?
Oldest sandhill on record: 36 years. Banded in '73,
Wyoming. Found again in 2010, New Mexico.

Lesser sandhills fly a thousand extra miles
to gather on the river, join the flock whose flyway
is older than rivers, older than memory.

Lesson 2: Historic metamorphosis.
In a strange land, cranes choose icy water, predator
deflection, blood flow slowed to stand the cold.

These places chosen by cranes,
places of safety, of meaning. For us,
offerings. Tracks we recognize.

Lesson 3: Portal. Cranes wait for south winds,
riding thermals, detecting the lengthening days.
Knowing when it's time.

At the library, the Stillwell documentary,
my row-partner peacefully sleeps
to the sound of sandhills.

Lesson 4: Migration. For what's been
re-arranged, outside and in:
We need to find those cranes.

Composed for the Cache Valley Sandhill Crane Festival
June 12, 2015, at Willow Park Zoo Education Building,
with thanks to Cindy Stillwell for her documentary film
shown at the Logan Library.

YELLOW YARROW

Yellow to gold from June through August, taupe in September,
Embers on umbels atop strawlike stalks gone spotted with mold,
Last of the summer's fickle weather.
Long days give way to sun red with smoke,
Old rituals of burning fields at harvest-end, the yarrow a border
Wanton and stubborn along the wire fenceline, hardy as cactus.

Yards and yards of yarrow-hedge, wide, profuse, sturdy
As the tech-industrial building glinting in slick siding
Rising just across the highway to the West,
Reflecting morning sun, sheen of steel and glass,
Omen at the start and end of every season,
Woven in the landscape, summer in the seeds, and fall.

Acrostic poem, composed September 2015; revised and presented for the Stokes Nature Center Gala poetry reading November 10, 2018.

POETRY IN THE DARK

In crisp November
on wind-sheltered bench,

a clutch of writers,
notebooks, flashlights.

Night plunges
down canyon walls,

Milky Way obscured
by the city's golden curtain

thrown across
a no-moon sky,

silhouettes of trees
rattling their shadows,

cougars parting grasses
in mass imagination,

old fears, metallic,
licking our cheeks,

falling into the river,
softening like leaves.

Hands pressed
to each other's,

a warmth
not expected.

As if eyes had been closed
and then opened.

Drafted during the Poetry in the Dark Walkabout Workshop at the Stokes Nature Center November 3, 2016, and presented at the Stokes Nature Center Gala November 10, 2018.

ALL THE BUTTERFLY MYTHS ARE TRUE

The Swallowtail that followed us
along a wooded trail for miles
one summer was, my sister said,
our father who died years ago,
returning to accompany his daughters
on our walk beside the stream
where butterflies touch down to fan
their wings, to revel in the cooling mud,
unbothered by our passing shadows.

Ancient Greeks and Europeans
thought a human dying takes the form
of butterfly, to pass through time,
to carry wishes. There along the forest path
we thought of Dad, his eager stride,
the way he made us laugh, the happiness
it caused to think of him as winged.

The human soul as butterfly?
No wonder Painted Ladies irrupt
spontaneous, millions on millions
washing over fields and highways
in waves of fluttering color,
all those eager spirits alighting
on thistles, nibbling the tender buds,
weaving their bedsilks into the leaves
where prickles protect their nests.

Some myths claim
butterflies
come back in human form,
a reason children believe
they can open their arms
and fly.

A reason to catch our breath
on narrow ridgelines
where dainty Cabbage Whites
flit among the mustards
as if to grant a wish.

Down along the streamside
a carpet of tiny blue butterflies,
color of flax, color of sky.

Butterflies as velvet. Butterflies
as flowers that fly and all but sing,
so saith Frost, a favorite poet.
Or butterflies as silence, as a cause
for us to ponder...butterflies.

Butterflies as dreams
brought forth in sleep, fragile
human souls in transformation,
in a series of transformations
until finally the soul
becomes a butterfly so pure
that when it dies...

And that is why we gather
milk weed pods in fall, their silk
and seeds a treasury for orange wings
we yearn to see each summer,
translucent panels like Tiffany glass
outlined in sleekest black,
the sheer fragility that opens
from chrysalises clinging to the common
milkweed plant, the one our father
let grow along the ditchbanks
on our family farm, knowing

how Monarchs would emerge
to unfurl their cloaks of silky fabric
tougher than skin, softer than breath.
Why not see the swarm, the rabble,
the kaleidoscope of butterflies
as human souls, not merely creatures
who find nutrients in mud,
but lift us and transform us
into finer spirits. Myths like seeds,
like dreams, the stories we need
to believe, as true as butterfly wings.

Composed and presented for the
Cache Valley Mariposa Festival at
the Gardener's Market on the county
courthouse plaza May 20, 2017.

OGDEN CITY WALKABOUT

Notebooks in hand, a swagger of poets,
Shadows on glass rising slick in the stormlight.

Concrete slaps shoe-soles, pungence wafts
Ripe from the deep out of black-iron grates.

Landscape once grass,
Repainted primordial gray.

Asphalt Amazon by order of the City
Where farmers once planted their fields.

Disked and then graded. A convoy of dump trucks.
Choice like a flower dried up, gone to seed.

Plastic flaps from overhead lines, a shaken mane,
The pure white lore of a pioneer's horse. Diaries.

Now poetry. Write wisdom, write legions of birds, write
Steel & brick, heavenly perfume flicking from dryer vents.

Write gold that lines the city-god's pockets; a pollen
Of truth waiting patient, salting the rosewood pews.

Poet as seeker, as signal, the sky
A shift for anything, unbuttoned, brisk.

Paper hearts braided, entwining, kites in the wires.
The long wait for substance and place.

Debris and devastation, the cusp of rotting lilac,
Sounds of children caged and searching.

Refusing to cut off their warrior braids,
Poets open like sunlight toward grace.

Compiled from words and lines of Star Coulbrooke, Anastasia Douglass, Morgan Ray, Jayrod Garrett, and Rees Sweeten, for the Writers at Work Poetry Walkabout Workshop in Ogden, Utah, April 14, 2018.

GROVE AND LAKE
    --for Nick, Joe, and Paul

Blessed Pando,
World's most ancient
Aspen grove,

May your succulence
Forever spread,
A trove of slender shoots

For beaver homes
Beneath the stillness
Of a young new lake.

Blessed lake,
Tributaries slowed
To caches

Where the beaver
Anchor aspen branches
For a midnight snack,

Beaver nestled
With their families
Underneath the ice.

Blessed pairing,
Beaver and Quakies,
Teeth and roots,

The pruning
And sprouting,
The water holding,

Control and release
For lodges and dens
Among aspen.

Blessed Beaver,
Creators of habitat,
Saviors of steams,

Of fish and of frogs,
Weasels, raccoons,
Herons that perch

Atop stick-built lodges,
Ducks on the pond,
Moose wading-in.

Blessed Pando,
Shall we fence out
Elk and deer and cows

And bring in beaver?
Task the beaver
Thirteen million pounds

Of clone to rescue,
To regenerate from drought
And beetles, pathogens,

The myriads of threats
To an organism with the heft
Of thirty-five blue whales.

(Did you know you can fake
A beaver attack on aspen
To get them to make seeds?)

(Did you know a beaver dam
Can co-exist with downtown
Parking lots in Walmart USA?)

Blessed scientists,
Pairing-up for answers
To the plight of Pando,

Stoking-up for stubborn
Little mammals, dam builders,
Tree-sprouters, lake-makers,

Partnering for habitat,
Living streams and troves
Of quaking aspen,

Blooming, spreading,
Channeling:
Riparian cultivation.

Bless our Wetland
Supercenters, better
Than a Walmart any day.

Composed and presented for the Bridgerland Audubon Society Spring Social, April 10, 2018.

DRIVING TO POCATELLO
--for Harald Wyndham
I

Up on the flat
    every April
        catching the freeway

through Idaho, lava fields,
    Russian Olives
        dotting ample farms,

rounding the big curve,
    hillsides rising
        to distant ski slopes,

taking the Clark Street Exit,
    Pocatello's old downtown
        across the tracks

where poetry waits in coffee shops,
    out-of-towners welcomed
        like prodigals,

microphone open
    to sweet-spot lines
        from northern Utah poets,

locals listening for intonations
    written from another state, another
        state of mind.

II

Twenty years arriving
    for the festival of writing,

                    Saturday nights
            at the Player's Warehouse,
                    theater of Beat,
black walls like the black
            wardrobe of poets
                    on hardback chairs
            below the stage,
                    drinks on the tables,

the poetry mascot mannequin
            decked-out and waiting
                    stoic, plaster-faced,
            for something profound
                    or funny to emanate
from pages shuffled, thumb-creased,
            licked and sorted
                    for a practiced,
            well-timed, hopeful delivery,
                    set to appeal,

set for shock-value, even,
            but nobody here
                    is shockable.
            A writer can say anything
                    in old-town Pocatello.

III

All those years
            driving to here,
where the writers are,

where Harald Wyndham,
            poet-publisher extraordinaire,
lays out his wares,

a tableful of Idaho titles,
        a coveted in-print imagining—
when will ours be there?

And then they were,
our words under Harald's
Blue Scarab imprint.

Harald, deep-voiced minister
        of poetry, dapper, trim
in black vest, black pressed shirt,

precious blue gem beetle,
        gold-inlaid, Bolo'd round his neck,
and a smile like the Portneuff Range,

with a great big invitation
        to be fearless.
Write like it.

IV

Drive like it.
        We drive to Idaho,
he drives to Logan,

this man, Harald,
        to read his poems,
bring his suitcase of books

for a program
        inspired by the Festival
he's been part of for decades.

And now he's going,
      moving away
to where nobody else
      is going, not yet,

so we're driving
      to a Farewell, driving
to Pocatello, one last time,
          for Harald.

Composed and presented at a farewell party for Harald Wyndham of Blue Scarab Press, June 22, 2016; revised and presented for the Memorial Reading at the Rocky Mountain Writers Festival, Pocatello, Idaho, April 14, 2018.

AT EIGHTY-TWO
--for Gino Sky

The poet's life is filled and hollowed.
As a poet, says the sage of poetry,
all the people you will ever know,

all those people with their trouble,
disillusionment and sorrow, they will
walk right through you.

As a poet, they will suck your marrow dry.

You will bear the world's
soreness, every illness,
all its bright and harrowing grief.

As a poet, every joy will be edged
with sharpened tines of what you know
too well to say out loud, but do.

Composed from a conversation with Gino Sky,
Pocatello/Salt Lake City Beat Poet, Nov.21, 2017.

BUDDHIST POET MEDITATES ON WATER
--for Michael Sowder

One hand plies the twin
oars
dipping starry water
black
as undulating night

He sees a face in deep-glass
lake
shimmering to age,
moon's plate its fractured
halo,
seaweed hair
wild in the background

Staring down the sorry
goblin
camped beneath the brick-arch
bridge,
oar-pusher aims his boat
through images
conjured and heretofore
unthreatening

Now the entry,
slotted, cavernlike, pulls him
deeper
into bottomless black water
deeper
than the mind's
release,
his boat a slip of light

Between sea and sky,
body and mind,
time and the end of it,
a pliant buoyancy

Composed at a City Art reading, Salt Lake City, Utah, Mar.13, 2016.

UTE LADIES'-TRESSES IN WETLAND PASTURE

Utah in summer
Turns wet, meadows
Emptied of winter.

Last of the snowpack
Advances its melt up the Wellsvilles,
Drowning the valleys
In pools lush with grass,
Emerald expanses dotted with color,
Serious buds ready to burst.

True to the Wetland,
Ripe, efflorescent, these delicate orchids
Emerge thin-stemmed, each blossom a chalice,
Succulent cups curving out, spiraling:
Spiranthus Diluvialis.
Elusive white stalks rise, ghostly
Surprises, one here, then one there,

Impish appearing
Next to the last one we spotted and marked.

With GPS in hand, the leader of our search
Eyes each ribboned stake we set beside
These rare endangered specimens,
Leopard frogs leaping past our feet
As we splash through grass, energized,
Not wanting to quit, this pasture a gift
Donated for study, anonymously.

Precious, the gift of conservancy.
Audubon volunteers counting each orchid,
Seeking to keep them from losing their meadow.
Tresses abounding in Mendon, on this thirty acres.
Utes weren't the first to appreciate
Rippled white cups braiding thin stalks. We observe
Each subsequent blooming and count ourselves lucky.

Acrostic poem composed for the Master Gardeners
"Conserving Rare Plants and Private Wetlands" event
on June 8, 2016, at Herm's Inn, Logan, Utah; published
on the Bear River Land Conservancy website, August 2017.

POEM FOR THE ONE AND ONLY DEAN JOHN ALLEN

November Four, the news
comes down by email,
first the usual
congrats and kudos,
progress of the College,
dreams we're building
for the future of our students,
money raised for scholarships,
for faculty promotions,
our hopes escalating
after years of legislative woe,
and then the blow:
Kathy and I, he's saying,
will move to the Oregon Coast.
I'll learn to walk
in sand, he says, without
my cowboy boots.

Picture this:
No cowboy boots, no dapper suit
with flat lapels that frame
a pastel shirt and classy
decorated tie,
pants pressed and hemmed
to perfect length, to ride
just right
atop the insoles of those boots,
to show the rise and set
of heel with every step as he
comes down the hall
at CHaSS or Ray B. West.

Instead, imagine
bare feet, shorts with pockets
full of rocks, of shells,
Hawaiian shirt unbuttoned, smile
so wide his white mustache
flips up, his sideburns flare.

Beside him, Kathy.
Behind him, nose bumping John's heels,
Cindy the horse.
On his other side Abraham, nudging
John's pocket for apples—
(oh, did I say that's his donkey?
And herding them all to keep the line moving,
Sage, the little Border Collie.

By July, he'll be fishing
on the coast,
coffee in hand, laughing
with Kathy
at lunch,
burgers and root beers
just like the old days,
high school sweethearts
dreaming
where life will take them.

Just like a John Wayne
movie
with gardening and poetry,
Aggie games
on TV, big glass full
of chocolate milk
and a sunset that spreads across
the whole universe,

his Oregon windows
lighting up
like his smile used to light up
Old Main.

Maybe one day
they'll get in the camper
(not Cindy or Abraham,
certainly Sage),
and drive out to see us
on Logan's high campus,
his favorites, the students
rushing to thank him.

Surely by then,
the beautiful building
we dreamed of together
will rise from the old
Ray B. West, with atriums,
porticos, cafes, a plaza
with fountains, technical
classrooms and parking garage.

We'll name it after him,
The John Allen Humanities Building,
make him stay in town
for one more celebration before
taking off his boots again
and walking in that white sand
like he's walking on the clouds,
a happy man.

Composed and presented for the retirement party
of John Allen, Dean of the College of Humanities
and Social Sciences, April 17, 2016.

CHRISTMAS BIRD COUNT

    --Cache Valley, 1955-2015, with thanks to Bryan Dixon

I

There's a window
you can do it in,
says Bryan, our Compiler.

There's a radius,
a fifteen-mile diameter
with Hyde Park in the middle,
specifically the Diet Coke machine.

There's a broad array of habitats
where we find a lot of species,
Heron, Egret, Baldpate, Shrike,
Towhee, Sparrow, Kingbird, Jay,
Grosbeak, Chat, Crossbill, Flycatcher—

such a winsome tongue twister
of old and new bird names,
brought to us with special thanks
to Dr. Archibald, the dentist
who became our first compiler
(the Diet Coke imbiber).

II

Back to Bryan:

There's a history of concern
for birds: dead birds on women's hats,
dead birds in curios, hundreds mounted
behind glass, preserved in all their colors,
thousands shot in just one day
of family sport, vacations called
for those who'd shoot the most before
a large elaborate Christmas meal.

And so, instead, we count them.
In Utah it began in Provo, 1904.
And now, says Bryan, 24
Count-Circles, all across the State.

In our fifteen-mile circle
there are sectors: mountains, fields,
sewage lagoons, even lowly
back-yard feeders. You can do it
from your own west window.

III

What you get from counting:

Audubon's mining the data, says Bryan,
for Climate Change reasons, migrations
shifting northward, coastlines deserted,
diseases that show up and why. Corvids
and West Nile, dying, resurging,
mysteries defined in the flight of birds.

IV

Why count in winter?

The Rough-Legged Hawk
comes down from Canada;
you won't see it here in summer.
Swainson's moves out;
Rough-Legged moves in.

You'll see Golden Eye Ducks
on first Dam, both kinds, and Hooded
Mergansers. Only in winter. Bush Tits
in Benson, and a Red-Necked Grebe.

V

After the count:

At six o'clock, a pot luck supper.
This is where the stories start:
those who've staked-out just one bird
for six weeks in advance, or those who
count the larger flocks by grouping
them, tens of tens, hundreds of tens,
rosy irruption of three thousand
finches, harmonic murmuration
of starlings, an iridescent cloud
of sixty thousand, gliding, whirling,
settling momentarily in treetops, bare
branches gone black with bird shapes.

VI

What's great about birding,
says Bryan, is birds are everywhere.

Deep in the maze of summer
or skimming the shimmer of winter,
birds. Out from the glass front curios,
back from the brim of milliners,
dodging the sheer sport shot gun,
windmill, skyscraper, car grill,
birds. You can see them from here.

If you're traveling for Christmas,
go to the Audubon website
and find the Count Circle near you.
Any day in that window will do.

Composed and presented for the Christmas Bird Count event at Willow Park Zoo, Dec. 9, 2015, with thanks to Bryan Earl for his interview with Bryan Dixon on Utah Public Radio's Zesty Garden program, Dec. 3, 2015.

BREATH, A CITY ART CENTO

I

A word can change sand into cloth—
      Mulchy ground, forest thunder, breaky thickets.

Say never, griever. Come, bereave;
      Hope will kill us ever.

Adjust, but slowly, the scented shape
      As yet unhoped, waiting in the front foyer

Wide aware. Losing it on every level.
      No wonder our tolerance has gone up.

II

Dragged into August, espaliered apples
      Hum closer and closer, nature and truth

Yielding to dreams, wilderness
      Devised, its stemmy prerogative;

Bees will hive, doves feast.
      This, the brambles, the monument,

The burning bush forgotten.
      Grasshopper shape in the clouds,

Promise in ambiguity:
      Weighted in favor of universe.

III

Revelation: Understand
    The suit, the self, the carapace

Opening like cages,
    Metallic and cool.

This coming season,
    Salvage the sweet-rot heat;

Look to the soft plump vines,
    Blessings born against the frost,

A mind gone slick, this breath—
    It all curls in on itself, in miniature,

In prayer, a smolder of features
    Tumbling to earth.

IV

One by fire, one who hit
    the teeming water,

One too weak, a botched heart.
    A craving, a symptom, a draped

Gold bloom of sweet silk ash,
    Thrashing.

Truth scored, the dark shell:
    Spiral of insight that goes too far,

Like an old leather wallet,
    Like silver-tailed rats.

Theft as poetic technique.
    A bad decade for God.

V

The tensile psychic filaments
    Pulse
In the city's struggling rumination,
    Itself so often a struggle,

Its ever-tightening scroll
    A minx in wisteria, listening,

Embroidered skull muttering mantras
    In a microphone, unflinching.

Find its rhythm-swooning patterns
    Fallen to the sea,

As if people grew from comfort;
    Died from ineffectual suspense.

Composed at the City Art Meltdown, Sept. 7, 2016, with words and lines from readings by Gerda Saunders, Kimberly Johnson, Wade Bentley, Pam Balluck, Lisa Bickmore, Sandy Anderson, Lynn Kilpatrick, Joel Long, Michael McLane, Jaqueline Osherow, Shanan Ballam, Natasha Saje, Laura Stott, Katharine Coles, Jennifer Tonge, Jerry VanIeperen, and Mike White.

FRY STREET FEBRUARY

    --Fry Street Quartet's performance of Franz Schubert and Benjamin Britten compositions for the Late Style Time and Experience concert at the NEHMA Museum & Music Series

Waves wander in lush circuits
    of our brains, our nervous
        systems, pleasant
pastoral visions film over dendrites,
    atoms, neurons, this music
        we're inside of
together,
    this room, these acoustics.

I sit next to Wulfgang,
    thirteen, with his ruler and paper,
        crossing his legs in the chair,
long hair flowing forward,
    this boy so fragile, so endearing,
        for we know his precarious
brainwaves, every moment
    a breath hold.

Rebecca McFaul, violinist, glosses the next
    composition, Britten's
late style, describing his grief and his frailty,
    then a pause, then the music
        suffusing the room,

and Wulfgang is still, quietly still,
        head in his mother's lap as she
lightly rubs his back,
      only his feet perceptibly peddling
          and flexing, to shunt
     the energy, nervous commotion.

But the music is hard breathing,
      heart-thumping, thrumming,
          reaching deep and sorrowful,
violins crying in keys so plaintive,
     so clear, so bird-like,
          full-storied and keening—

The violins plink and sing, the cello
      throat-hums, thrums, moans—

All hesitate, a silent breath,
      musicians hold—then turn the page,
        another seamless shine
    of such inimitable sheening,
oh such pristine high sound,
      high and woodbine,
   stringline, hightine—

There it goes. We're all going,
     We are in this weird place
         inside-above-into
    the sound that is surreal,
        in-the-room-of-the-room
    beside the body of each of us,
        sitting tangibly next to us,

Wulfgang dreaming, lifted in the music
      with the rest of us,
his mother's hand poised, gently, gently
      in the turning teeming notes—
We are breathing together, audible,
      our blood, our cells, our souls,
          art bouncing off the sheen
      and shoals of soundwaves
          washing into us, pulling back
      and crashing in again, emotions, emotions,
          deep and deep and moving—
We cannot but move to it, hearts filling,
      filling, sighing, breath, time, rising,
          a trembling knowing being,
      a lace, an embroidery in the air.

Composed at the Nora Eccles Harrison Museum,
Utah State University, Logan, February 24, 2019,
for Rebecca McFaul, Robert Waters, Bradley Otteson,
and Anne Francis-Bayless, for their life-altering music,
and also for Wulfgang and his mother, Becca Johnson,
for the strength of their love.

OF BALANCE AND GRACE:
THE PUBLIC FACE OF LEADERSHIP

   --A Tribute to USU President Noelle Cockett

There are those who make
each person
in this turning   teeming world

believe that they are worth
the salt   the work

    the true   regard
afforded to a dignitary—

how it feels   to be held
in such   esteem—

Every person matters,
        she says softly.

    This is the woman who
    takes off her shoes
    and hands them to one
    who likes her style,
    wears her size, the high
    strappy heels they both love.

    This is the woman who
    breastfed her baby at work
    when she was graduate dean,
    who showed her students
    they could be moms and scientists
    both at the same time.

This is the woman who
tries something new every year
in the garden, the woman who
sequenced the sheep genome.
Who would have known
a Montana ranch girl
could grow into CEO?

It isn't male versus female,
she insists. It's abilities and strengths
and asking for help when you need it.

> This is the woman who
> asks every person, all of us,
> to share what she's inherited
> and grow it into something
> firm and nourishing as new tomatoes
> harvested from her own garden.
>
> Over that shared harvest,
> she may tell us how she met her
> sweetheart between rugby and lacrosse,
> how she visited her parents
> in Oahu every year, how she loves
> hosting parties, loves her mom
> and sisters, loves her cats,
> her husband, and driving very fast.
>
> Her friends and colleagues
> will say she is free of judgment,
> accepting of others, a skier
> who carried her kids on her back,
> who is always engaged intellectually,
> who can give a speech
> without notes, without prep,

        who is vital to her field.

Even with that measure
      of intense   and varied
life   experience
how does one aspire,

transpire   to such   a height?

        This is the woman who
        transformed
        a university's history—

        and is changing it softly,
        committed to its best aspects,
        asking of it, and of us, a better balance.

How many of us know

how much   it takes
to gain   that kind   of grace?

Composed and presented for the Inaugural Celebration of the new USU president, May 4, 2017. Published in Utah State online and print magazine, Fall 2017.

THE GODS

In language, there are assumptions,
Definitions
We don't understand.

Maybe the world has no lessons,
No meaning
To articulate, the stories we tell
Meant to be changed
With the telling.

Good stories bend, like snakes.
Driven from under,
They seep out in stars, sun, water,
Form bodies of color.

Yellow, blue, white.
Wind blows them backward,
Turns their fan-blades,
Their vivid intentions.

Words trip on wire,
The dirty glass door,
The dog,
Which is god,
Its death a non-language.

Endure the live harvest,
Killed quail hung in rows
On barbed fences,
Bones splayed, corrugated.

Story begs no explanation.

You guess, you wait, you tell it later.
You wait as long as it takes,
The world bending its shape,
Until the story you tell comes true.

Ars Poetica, composed after a poetry reading
by Russ Winn at Helicon West July 28, 2016;
revised and presented for the USU English
Department Faculty Retreat August 17, 2017.

LAMENT OF AN AGING BOOKWORM

Can't get down to the dirt
of reading. Can't get under
the surface of words
to mine their subtle ironies.

The passages I most admire
don't nestle deep enough to stick.

I'm out of the habit of delving
with gusto, retaining the gist,
innuendo, the current
too deep, too muddy and swift.

Images thrash in my brain,
shedding dimension.

Each time I set the book down,
the slate is wiped clean.
Each time I pick the book up,
I have to go back to begin.

All I thought I knew
is dried at the synapse,
not rooted in my mind.

Oh I wish I could keep
the strange exciting elegance
of phrasings I once relished,
then forgot.

Composed and presented for the Logan Library
Quarterly Membership Meeting, July 8, 2015.

LOVE SONG FOR STAN LEROY ALBRECHT

    --after "The Love Song of J. Alfred Prufrock, with a nod
    to the Fab Four

I: What he Carries

You see him stride the crosswalk
on Champ Drive, easy in his manner
like the Beatles on that album cover,
Abbey Road, that bell-bottom flare,
that equanimity of purpose.

He's alone, rare occurrence, on his way
to catch a plane, make a speech, entice
another million-dollar donor for the school.

See him. All that weight he carries
on his shoulders, in his face—
and yet, the look is tender, one part
worry, one part sorrow, two parts joy.

Remember he's the voice of campus,
every careful conversation, every soul
considered. Fortunate, this album cover picture
pressing itself into memory, easing
the missing you know is coming.

    Let him go then,
    where the evenings are peach and coral,
    where the rock art spreads its ancient code
    across the high plateaus—

II: How He Finds Balance

The hazy summer air of Logan rubs its shoulders
on the buildings, on the windows of campus,

a five-minute drive to where he plants his garden
in a hoop house early spring,
sets the tender starts as soon as students
in the high schools set their sights on USU.

No time to linger in work his hands favor,
a thousand decisions to make on funding, on buildings,
on weighing the whims of a legislature.

    His mind is as perfectly pressed as his slacks.

In between, he dreams of Buelingoes,
the Oreo cows he pastures in Fremont, home
of his childhood, calves cavorting like kids
playing Frisbee. His cabin awaiting
retirement, First Lady Joyce at his side.

    In the classrooms students come and go,
    talking of Brandywine tomatoes.

III: When and Where He's Going

Indeed there's time; there will be time.
This summer, fishing in Alaska,
all the halibut he can eat, thrill of a catch
filleted for the freezer. Winters in Florida,
not just a week off and on, but as long
as he likes.

    There will be time
    once the Regents decide a replacement.

Time for work until then, moments with his
wife, his daughters, moments when
the visions and revisions of a lifetime

are rewarded in the long eventuality
of leaving, when they will step out of this role.

    Worth it,
        after all, though we hate to see them go.
If we could rub a magic lantern
and a clone of Stan appear—and Joyce—but no.
We let them dare to eat that peach,
we hear them singing, each to each,
Jimmy Buffet on the stereo and baseball
in the anteroom, strains of Margaritaville.
And pizza. Any kind, any place.

There will be time to linger in Wayne County,
fishing pole in hand, Oreo cows in the pasture.

    Let them go then, Stan and Joyce,
    where the evenings are peach and coral,
    where the rock art spreads its ancient code
    across the high plateaus—
              and oh, the fishing is fine.

Composed and presented for President Stan Albrecht's
retirement event August 2016, with thanks to Syd Peterson.

IN THE HALF LIGHT

Birthing new, every glade,
    every waterfall,

brooding gods of clouds moving
    over all,

the thickets, the water,
   the rising yellow glaze
    of morning

unravelling the creeks
   over rocks that roll
     with treasure,

burst of winged creatures
     to fish with,

dream of a trout
     hunting in shallows,

crimson gill plate,
    anvil head,

cut
  throat.

Drafted at a reading by Chadd VanZanten
for Helicon West, from his essay
"No Caution in Them," Sept. 14, 2017.

KAREN

picks me up for lunch
in her big old Riviera,
low-slung frame, sleek interior,
seats that lay you back
when she steps on the gas.

Karen

walks like a model,
hips leading, legs fluid,
a saunter that carries her
luxury-like, time enough to talk
while flashbulbs pop the runway.

Karen

wears her classy pinstriped
slacks, a pretty blouse
with lace, her too-thin frame
belied by cancer's hard return,
the softness in her face.

Karen

with her history of surgery;
you wouldn't know it,
sense of humor sharper
than the knife she's been under
most of her life, scars you can't count.

Karen

smiles like there's no worry,
says she can't decide quite yet

about the transplant, marrow
not making blood cells, spleen
swelling, liver next to go.

Karen

says, "Let's drive the long way
home, the day's so beautiful."
You look at her as if angels
are real and music of the spheres
plays in her hands, on her grand piano.

Composed for Karen E. Erickson, Apr. 21, 2016; published in her Memorial program, August 7, 2016.

WISDOM FROM THE EDGE OF ALZHEIMER'S

--For the residents and staff of the Sunshine Terrace

I went to college at forty with a scholarship,
thanks to the CEO of a workplace where value
is measured in patients and family and staff,

where a Certified Nurse's Aide can go on
to get a degree while caring for those
who've forgotten more than she'll ever know.

Wing 1, August 31, 1992

Martha knows, somehow, I've had decisions
to make. She takes an assessment, gives her advice:
Education comes first. Don't let him stop you.

Wing 1, Sept. 20, 1992

Rosy has her glow on, cheeks as pink as her name,
smiling through pain, cooing as if for a baby she holds,
remnant of memory as real for her as the daughter
she doesn't know, the daughter who visits her daily.

Wing 1, Oct. 31, 1992

We're watching a TV Western with captions,
Where men die young and women die lonely,
when gentle Viola speaks up. *A woman can sit
in the shed with the cows and be less lonely
than when her man's around. I've been there.
I know what I'm talking about.*

I wonder where that spunk was hiding
before our shy Viola told it like it was.

I wonder how it is that Martha knew
I had to divorce to go back to school.

I wonder at the secret in Rosy's smile
as I take her dishes from my cupboard,
gift from her daughter after she died,
pink rose pattern, a setting for each aide.

What does it cost for those families
whose loved ones disappear
in the smoke of stolen memory,

whose brilliance burns down to the barest
wisdom, accessible only in moments of clarity
fleeting as clouds in a September sky?

I remember that late September
when we loaded the green bus from Wing 1
and drove up the canyon to see the leaves,
windows open to the autumn breeze,
Viola sweeping her hand across her cheek
to brush a wisp of silver hair as it drifted
over her eyes, her smile of contentment so rare,
a thing to cherish, even with its hint of sorrow.

Even in sorrow, that smile.

Composed and presented for the Cache County
Walk to End Alzheimer's, September 9, 2017.

FACING FEARS

We didn't know
We'd have to reinvent ourselves,
Move from twilight sleep
Of hidden grief
Into memory's sharp persistence.

For years, we've ached to write,
To speak. Repressed, mistrusting
Those we loved,
The few who could have helped us
But did not.

The Chrysalis of past injustice
Cracks, and we emerge,
Stronger, wiser, confident.
These are our words,
The instruments of our resistance:

Fears, filling the sky—
Leap over, go through?
Give me your hand; we're not alone.

Man of true endeavor
Knits a tender gift, needles and yarn
His redefinition.

Mom in the workplace,
Dad in the ambulance—
Paint us their happier endings.

Beautiful colors so delicate,
Fluttering, rising,
Innermost wishes free on the wind.

Heaven in a pure, true hug.
Touch that dissolves trouble.
Sturdiness a form of beauty.

Questions that bring light, a dawning—
Why not women, why not life,
Why not peace?

Love that keeps enduring
Every day for forty years
Through every kind of sorrow.

Goddess of dreams, lavender fields,
A waltz with the fireflies.
Hours melting to honeydew.

Compiled from words and lines written by participants in the Women and Gender Studies Faculty Luncheon in a writing exercise following my talk, "Reviving the Dream of a Common Language: Poetry for a Troubled World" presented at the USU Alumni House on April 5, 2018.

Contributors:
Anne Hedrich, Ace Beorchia, Alexa Sand, Eddy Berry, Michelle Hixson, Patricia S. Moyer-Packenham, Diane Alston, Ann Austin, Celina Wille, Madeleine Soule, Kathy Chuboda, Julie Foust-Andrew, Lynne McNeill, Robert Heaton, Brionne Neilson, Mollie Murphy, Claudia Schwabe, Becca Johnson, Susan Andersen, Lidia Delgado, Alex Anthony Johnson.

ME TOO

Of the actual experience, from which do I write?
Psyche, or heart?

They say the heart's call won't matter to many
Unless it's set forth in image,

The blue-black center of muscle pulsing,
Viscous red cells clinging together,

Shunting through ropey veins under the skin,
Curling and forking,

Backs of the hands, crease of the elbows,
Your tender and toughened jugular

So easy to sever. Of the heart, though, where
Does experience reside?

We say we can't write it in blood, though sometimes
We do.

Written for the students of Dr. Christine Cooper Rompato in her English 2600 class, April 23, 2018.

SAYING IT

They say the heart's call won't matter to many
Unless it's set forth in image,

The blue-black center of muscle pulsing,
Viscous red cells clinging together,

Shunting through ropey veins under the skin,
Curling and forking—

But saying it outright, the swift slap of words,
The crack at the edge of silence: that's where it counts.

Be a force of nature, your own nature. Be sassy.
Open those intricate folds where destruction lay hidden.

Hurt but defiant, confront the past, the demons of freedom,
Though knees shake, hands tremble, sweat beads.

For what happens when you can't say what you see
And think and hope? Records of frustration.

In love and loss, forget the fear, meet everyone,
Hear everyone, see everyone. Find the words to say.

Avoidance is a distant stranger, accidental eye contact,
A kitchen knife that dulls and sharpens, full of wear.

Be the songs that burst with power, break the silence,
Smash the terror with emotion, passion, laughter.

No more hushed tones, no worry. Time to insist: Look at me,
Pay attention to me, I have something to say!

Compiled from words and lines written by Dr. Christine
Cooper Rompato's students in English 2600, April 23, 2018.

Contributors: Nikole King, Sadie Leonhardt, Shylee Wheeler,
Zack Schenk, Madison Lang, Danni Noyes, Andraea Shelley,
Breanna Lovell, Hannah Smith, Samantha Mace, Amy Graham.

THE WITCHES DANCE

On Center Street, three dozen witches
step inside the intersection,
brooms and scepters raised to setting sun,
traffic stopped, the headless horseman
galloping inside their circle,
clearing space for crowds of people
costumed, waiting, kids in hand,
anticipation building, music flooding
from the speakers where a gated home,
historic, opens itself to the macabre,
the celebratory, and the witches begin,
turning and stamping and moving
their sleek-dressed hips to the beat
of a high-volume thumping that pulls
the crowd in, cheering and breathless
at once, this circle of witches pulsing
with energy, hats pointed, boots tramping,
witches of lavish description
pounding the ground with scepters
and brooms, raising them high, a joyful
excursion of costume and festival.

Almost as soon as the dance has begun,
it comes to an end. The witches pretend
to be regular people in Halloween garb,
partying together as the trick-or-treaters
line up at historic houses now open
to cauldrons of candy, grandmother witches
seated in entries, handing out treats
to wide-eyed little monsters and fairies
and baby witches there with their parents,
lined-up all the way out to the street
where the witches have just finished dancing.

And the moon at three quarters
is noticed by partiers to be a blue one,
truly a light blue, a slight smoky haze
moving over its face as it rises southeast
of the houses and glasses of cider and wine
raised to toast witches who carry the crowd
to a high they will bring back again
every year at Halloween on Center Street,
the Witches Dance.

Composed for the annual Center Street event in Logan,
for Richard, Teri, Robert, and Barbara Guy, Nov. 1, 2017.

AMANDA, AMONG THE BONES

Premise:

One year to remember
    everything.

        Rattling footbridge
            meadow snow
                sun on the deer—

In waist-high grass
    hands on hips,
    this boy, this lost watch.

Corrosion.

Buried halfway, mounded,
    all the humans
        gone to rust,
a pile of rags, of sinew, heat-dried
    skin, no one you could fathom.

Looking, looking,
    you look for Ruby
and Valentine,
    red-pout lips,
a boy who might live
    past the last inoculation.

You write about
        bones so your own son
    arrives and arrives,
        one dream
        to the next.

Then, a silhouette,
    a scraggle of fist,
    deflection of stride,
        clamp of iron wrist—

This is how
    the boy will rise
        into being
    only months before the end.
  .

Oh beautiful, oh
    meadow mother, decades
parse the grass,
    tread the water,
cross the bridge—

Rising up from buried earth,
your prodigal
    will recognize
        the bones
that parted
    for his birth.

The watch, the bloody rust,
the silhouette—
    this meadow
    where you found him
    in a spray of black letters
    on the pages of your book.

Composed and presented at a reading by Amanda Luzzader at Helicon West, Feb. 14, 2019.

WHAT BEN SAID

I

Got some readers who could see
      Inside the scar on his
          Forehead
Collected drops of red
      Words slung in blooms
          One after another
Gutted, shot, snapped
      In halves and quarters

Readers to balance, re-balance
      All the meanings
          Wet and blinking
Falling breech against the page

He lived in Milwaukee
      Only one enemy
      Chained, scraping
      The Sunday streets
Never ashamed, never tamed
      Of childhood
      Asleep in the wrap
          Of light
A match-whoosh, torch
      Of paper wasp nest

Already at the middle
      Incredibility
      Of life so far

When his wife is taken, weeping
    And his ars poetica
    Has gone to cats
Cats that kill—
    Slap, piss, forgive—

The Marriott blazer,
The tall tall daughters,
The conference genre,
The academic restlessness.

And then he's on
    To the natural world
    To the cattails, hawks, and ripples
Of a lyrical sunlit swell

II

Oh Ben, you notice
    The novice of reading the earth
Its human-mottled moldings
    Bordered, bridged
        Freewayed

Raise us like the sonnet
    You sacrifice
    To night and a slight
        Thin girl
Pure, fierce, dream-machining
    Her syncopated
        Halt
Her random click-around
    To where death
        Becomes
            Escape—

Escape to the last section
      Crying in the wind
          Salt-skinned
      Groaning
Staring us down.

New poems.
From randomly reading online.
To prove that he's doing
SOMETHING on Sabbatical.

III

Warmed, Woke
      The experiment ended
      Participants Kevlar'd
      Trickle of ash
Lifting the plank of their bodies
      Rank sweat

Found equals Heart
      Remains peeled away
Oh cut, oh pare
Oh positive talk

      Imagine delicate pain
      Imagine direction
          Lakes back-waved

No microphone
      No lock, no stand

      Little sexy sweat moves
Come-hither
      In the dark

      Oh Prince, oh Purple
           Oh Red Corvette—

He's done the James Brown
      He's done the Elvis
      Gyre, jump, jive

      Nothing left in his pockets
           But sonnets.

Composed at a reading from *Welcome, Dangerous Life* by Logan author Ben Gunsberg at Utah State University Merrill Cazier Library, January 29, 2019.

FIRST DANCE
    —for Dani and Jeremy

To find the one you love,
    your first and only:

Met in church
    where she taught
        dance, Scottish-Irish, each dancer
            in formation on their own.

First time he came to class
    he was smiling, he was quiet, she was nervous,
        he the first guy to show up.

    She knew he just wanted to dance:
        Ballroom in high school,
        Folk dance in college,
        performed twenty years
        in China, in Haiti, Nauvoo—

She'd been dancing all that time,
    ever since she was ten, in festivals, yes,
    all over the west, and she'd taught only girls.
    Until now.

Back up:

    First time they met, a medieval event.
    She was playing Chess. Didn't know how
        to play Chess. He was standing
            off in a corner, meeting her eye,
            giving her hand signals, which move
            to make.

He proposed in Seattle, on the ferry,
    city lights and all, such a romantic.
    She's no romantic.
When you find love,
    you know it.
        Deeper than romance,
            deeper than dance.

    She knew he would ask, just didn't know
        when.

    They're so different, night and day:
        He's Sci-Fi and fantasy; she's journalism;
        he the long novel, she the short story.

            At the core, though, they're the same:
            Writing, dancing, family.
            They both want six kids.

Correction:

    First time they met,
        they didn't really meet, both
        at a performance, out of town,
            100 dancers, five years ago,
        how funny to think of it now.

She danced ballet, did Yoga training,
    bought him a mat for Christmas.

    He liked it.

How she decided she really liked him:
When she asked what he wanted
in the future, he said, I want
community, a place to meet. To dance.

She knows he likes the waltz, but she doesn't do
partner dancing. Tonight, her group will dance
without her.

Tonight, she'll dance her first waltz.

When they settle down,
what they both want: a home
with a barn in the back
for dancing.

Written and performed for the wedding
of Dani Hayes and Jeremy Gohier at the
Elite Hall in Hyrum, Utah, Mar. 1, 2019.

LETTER TO A FRIEND
FOUR MONTHS AFTER SUICIDE

Dear Joshua Lew

I was walking in a pasture
when it turned to deep water

flooding swirling
everywhere I turned

I grabbed onto the corner of a splintering
barn and kicked my legs in the murky lagoon
until they lifted free

and I was flying up at the end of a long
streamer like his long hair
and I saw his eyes

as kind and lost as they were
before we lost him

and I almost thought
he was back again
writing

and reading with that soft
voice

the one we never thought
we could lose and we haven't

not yet

I still hear it over the swirl and moan
of the deep deep water

Written for Joshua Lew McDermott
in memory of Tyler Esplin, April 2019.

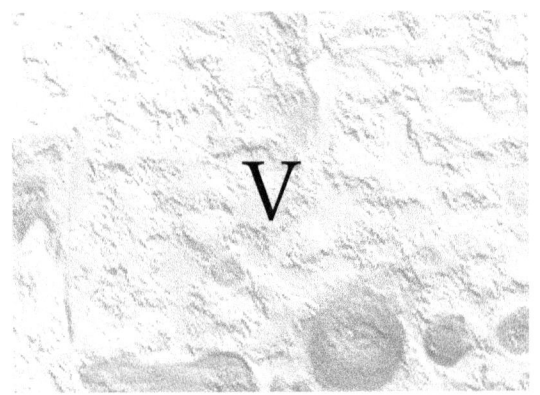

SEASONS IN THE CITY OF POETRY

I

Under summer shadow
of the comforting oak

we drift,
enveloped in warmth,

ravens spiraling, primary feathers
thrusting skyward, flamenco dancer fans
disappearing against the blue.

Summertime seeps like water
rolling off plump rounded bodies of raspberries,
sweet things bending to memory:

afternoons we spent as children
stretching into age,
dressing in dim stardust.

II

Twin white pinnacles
thrust their spires
through lowering El Greco skies,

thin streams of sunlight
dancing from tree branches, yellow jackets
swamping fountains of blue water.

We look up, remember
day after day of rain,
and recognize
the season has changed.

No sound, no sense of being,
no movement of air,
just the falling away forever,
one petal, then another,

fragments out of time,
incongruous
against the cityscape,
the cafés and theaters,
hardware stores.

III

Rotation of clouds
through high atmosphere,
the vivid, vital force of winter:

Willow trees touched by arctic winds
transform to fountains of thin, silver glass.

Weighted with ice, power lines
dip, sway, ring like plucked strings.

Then freshly fallen snow remakes everything
in pristine softness, smooth and deep.

Another December skating party,
another white sky gone gray.

Teased by tropical dreams
of January thaw, we trod
through a month-long inversion,
remind ourselves
it's temporary.

IV

We want to hold a sign
saying
DO NOT ENTER,
because sometimes
the world can hang so heavy.

Instead, we
hold one saying
WELCOME
to this new season of serenity.

We hold a place for those
who arrive,
never questioning their right
to stay.

We don't know how they felt,
those who came before us,
though we've sat on the same
screened porch

watching red maples scatter long rays
of the setting sun

until the trees outside our windows
grow heavy with snow
and a longing for spring.

V

Hear the spring birds
twinkling in the branches,
their voices like starlight.

See the crocus forcing its bright candle,
see the willow goldening.

Barren boughs of March
host little ripples of bud-break,
sweet green progeny glimmering
against a calico sky.
How tall, how resilient
the sea of tree tops in April,
interlaced branches, everything green,

then blossoms. Blossoms alive
with the warm, wet buzzing of bees.

When they're through, we look up in surprise
at the petalfall.

VI

Here on the river's edge
the trees are heavy with contentment,
arching their thick leafy arms over berries
and sedge, shading the supple grass.

Summer sun lights up the mountains,
unfurls weathered scrolls of recall.

It's then we realize and maintain
everything is beautiful.

Morning light raises the faces of sunflowers,
the stubborn ones Nature loves,
the willful seeds, determined roots.

The flowers lean, the sun moves on
not looking back or down.

Meanwhile, there's no fear
of being left behind, no angry spirits
pointing spears,
just the endpoint of Eternity
in sapphire skies.

So little is expected
to fly through to joy.

A Collaborative, Commemorative, Community Poem
created from lines written by participants of the Logan
Poetry Walkabouts, 2015-16, presented to Mayor Petersen
and the Logan City Council August 16, 2016.

Contributors:
Star Coulbrooke, Sabine Barcatta, Shanan Ballam, Shannon Branfield, Riley Burke, Helen Cannon, Gail Christensen, Jessica Christiansen, Brock Dethier, Lisa Duskin-Goede, Terysa Dyer, Kat Farrow, Jordan Floyd, Mary Ellen Greenwood, Chloe Hanson, Anne Hedrich, Danny Howell, Brooklynn Knight, Luke Lemmon, Iris Nielsen, Winona Perry, Justin Peterson, Alyssa Quinn, Felicia Rose, Amias Shipley, Aaron Timm, Isaac Timm, Millie Tullis, Charles Waugh, Alexa Aho West, Maria Williams, Thomas Worthen, Robert Woodbury.

SEASONS IN THE CITY:
WILD WISE NATURE

"All you people gathered here,/
Do you have some words that sear?"

The way of the world's energy—
    wavering, flickering like candles
revealing truth
    in leaves of aspen, clouds
    cumulous white,
evening primrose
    pinked with sunset,
mirror of geese in purple dusk.

Each season offers itself
    like an unopened box,
mystery and memory
    in growth's own time,
blossoms flooding the air
    with wild aroma,
blackberries bursting,
    willow reaching barren fingers
to a sky laced with fire,
    summer's last pale children
        clinging.

In the city, wooded spaces
    load our senses with deliberate intent,
leaves shuffling near coffee-dark river,
    stones half-crossing the bed.
Above us, panther shedding lightning
    from its black-cloud underbelly,
ravens filling winter sky
    with raucous sharpened wings.

The poet knows: Go not gently.
    Swirl, plunge, leap, and twirl.
Fall, bombastic shouts of leaf.
    Shatter, breath of lake receding,
molecules of water bursting,
breaking against softness, sticky sweet
    from nature's whimsy.
    Human will: a hot cast iron searing
    barest palm. Lean into it.

No slumbering away our sadness,
    no summer unrelenting,
no steel clouds grave and mute,
    no shards to shower down
to bleed the words from secret places.
    No suspending trust, no fearing
tyranny when nature brings us tulips.

    Let us wear wonder like a tattoo.
Let emotion become beauty,
    let it ring out like Beethoven,
let it tumble as on fluttering wings that veer
    and reverse in chaotic, perfect unison.

This time of year, we're called to the wild
    by late summer cricket song, cool dew
on the lawn, crisp essence of being alive.
    This time of year, birds hold up
the lowering clouds, their flashing eyes
    reflecting yellow trees against dark sky.
Bees condense into clouds of sweetness,
    heart-pumping, fast-moving beings
that terrify like sudden love.

This time of year, we can't help forecasting
    a brittle winter, solstice stars glittering,
rivers rounding their silver into icy baubles,

      letting them go like lanterns.
Cold finds our weak spots, slips under our shirt,
      brushes the spine at the back of our
                                neck.
Before it licks our faces, dwell here, in the now.

Be beautiful, be still in the wild of nature,
      the soul of the city, eternity compressed.
This delicacy of beauty splashes all over us.
      We hold worlds waiting to be told,
each twig and root. A comfort to know:
      there are candles burning everywhere.

A Collaborative, Commemorative Community Poem created from lines written by participants of the Logan Poetry Walkabouts, 2016-17, presented to Mayor Petersen and the Logan City Council Aug. 15, 2017

Contributors:
Star Coulbrooke, S. K. Anderson, Shanan Ballam, Alan Blackstock, Amy Blakely, Luz Maria Carreno, Carly Crosby, Brock Dethier, Meg Dice, Bryan Dixon, Lisa Duskin-Goede, Terysa Dyer, Bonnie Glass-Coffin, Heather Griffiths, Tara Hawkins, Joshua Hortin, Patrick Huffcutt, Emily James, Kristin Ladd, Pam Loosle, Jean Lown, Kasondra Payne, Bruce Pendery, Paul Rogers, Hilary Shughart, Aaron Timm, Isaac Timm, Sarah Timmerman, Millie Tullis, Jim Wheeler, Sarah Ann Woodbury.

POEM FOR WHO WE ARE

A people, close inside the valley's soul,
in the copper light of summer.

What binds us together is fragile,
people breathing hurt or joy
or something in between,
tossing down our offerings
the color of bruised plums,
a lavender wideness in our eyes.

We are dreamers of a better way,
navigating by feel, by emotion,
writing words of tufted softness
that drift on the current like grief,
like leaves relieved of their dry,
brittle crunch.

We are people of desert and forest
seeking to know our place
in a land
once meadow grass and dragonflies,
people whose tiny alterations
can change life on a grand scale,
umber sky burning earlier and earlier.

People whose elders
were once castaways
shuttled from shelter to home
who were patient and lived long
and cached their descendants away

in the eventual safety
of this northern Utah hamlet.

People whose minds
were shiny black and sharp as flint,
their stories full of loop and flop,
words glowing glorious,
peach button sprouts, birds' heartbeats.

People welding pen to paper,
words glistening and snapping
like live-wire bouquets.

People who've waited
for that phone call
in the middle of the night, dreading
what might come next
though everyone they know
is tucked safe
underneath their roof.

People who walk with the weight of sky
held Atlas-like, bearing the objects of Earth,
summer tombstones, clouds of silver gnats
and dreams of democracy dying.

People ferocious with power,
who take up their pick ax, their armor,
to shatter the loneliness,
break down the battlements
used to exclude,
like children playing spooners with the outcasts,
chucking spoons not rusty knives,

children who don't have to try
to believe, to be caring, to matter.
People are their wooden mansions,
are the green of branches they walk under
in the whethers of unwieldy weather,
are the book and paper, friend and first kiss,
games of shadow tag, the darting
and the weaving and the choosing of a life.

We are rare symbolic squares
of cloth sewn into little packets
and clipped to the limbs of an old majestic elm.
We are the surging joy of ivy,
sidewalk art of breezy leaves,
our quirky personalities, our knowledge
and its loss, how summer lasts all year
in the longing for it, and our lives will sooner
than later be elevated to ash.
Meanwhile, the bus that rolls along
our city streets will always take us in,
hopeful grandparent, hopeful child,
tracing together with colored chalk
the uncertainty of what lies ahead.

Confusion on the cusp of change
means reaching out to shape the words
that yearn. Polite and steady, brought to life
in scratches and swoops,
they line up to serve us, we who persist
as lichens persist, free dancing,
photosynthetic, we the clean air indicators,

habitat ingratiaters, standing with the children,
deferring right-of-way.

Inside we are islands, tentacles
in the solar current, blastocytes revolving
through memories of water and thunder,
our oil-slicked prayers rising
on the surging hope of Future.

We are, at the end of the day,
just needing to be loved, just trying
to get home, in this city of who we are,
this town that lifts us to one tribe.

A Collaborative, Commemorative Community Poem created from lines written by participants of the Logan Poetry Walkabouts, 2017-18, presented to Mayor Daines and the Logan City Council Aug. 21, 2018.

Contributors:
Star Coulbrooke, Nathan Allen, Kendall Becker, Brenda Brunello, Ryan T. Choi, Gail Christensen, Trekton Christiansen, Chris Davis, Brock Dethier, Valerie J. Downs, Terysa Dyer, Natalie Fjeldsted, Alisha Geary, Mary Ellen Greenwood, Anne Hedrich.

LOVE POEM TO LOGAN CITY

I

Cradled in the valley a delicate sea
of color and movement,
mountains against it, eagles above,
sun pouring golden yolk, plying
its honeyed peach, lily pink simmer,

no wonder we love
descending from canyons, returning
to sun-lit yards with lilac trees
and dragonflies,
burble of water, burble of voices
familiar in topic and timbre,

no wonder we love
recounting old memories of rosebushes,
carrots, a treehouse, wild roses
baby pink and wanton
spilling over concrete walls,
the wind as it drags its silver hair
of rain across the sky,

the subterranean reach of aspen root,
pale boles holding fast the fading light
as smoke drapes the mountains,
wreathes gauzy white arms around spires
and peaks, marries the sky of murky steel blue
to orange-gold sunset, flames
licking the sagebrush slopes,
these rust and coral bones under earth's skin,
the glittering sand of our lives,
this one small moment in time.

II

Nestled in the center
of a burgeoning oasis
fed by its namesake river,
Logan settles deep in the belly
of summer, air gone humid
and thick with ripened berries,
butterflies in our bellies.

Our hands moving over its surface
for decades, this place
formed by time is transformed
to a heaven of houses and gardens,
sunlight reflected through the crabapple tree,
Lily of the Valley wafting
its secret perfume, tiny blooms
shining like pearls in the shade.

With our hands we have harnessed the river,
petted and parted it, spread its long locks
over Juniper knolls, turning the sagebrush
to garden's random wander,
sweet pink clover like stars in the grass
sparkling in high desert sun.

In a million years, if the river
is still running in low calm
or brutal bashing, it will still be speaking
depths untouched by any of us,
the tumult and long mean
lashings of run-off leaving blood-brown
canes of roses beat by liquid life,
absorbed by earth.

Still, we have loved it. Heavy
with the invincibility of childhood
we have chiseled and sanded this place
with patience, shaped it into something new,
we who've learned to listen
for the thrum of centuries, the high thin
keening of our vanishing.

Right here in this moment in all our comforts,
we do not sink. We lean into it
in abiding love, our infinite hearts linked.

III

Logan your story is set in stone,
geologic in scope, filled with curious things,
granite chips culled from abandoned
quarries buffed into smooth glossy shine,
sandstone cliffs embracing in the sunset,
humans hungering for gold.

We are chinking in the slats of your house
blown open by the crush of time,
our stories passed on in the color of hair,
noses, long fingers, our selves passed down
with words pulled from the family graveyard
and a feeling too big to contain,
stories to make us immortal.

We stand in our too short time, each
generation holding the next one steady,
holding energy, the power to heal.
Like crystals frozen deep in time,
we arise fresh and new from the mantle,
resplendent with the light of day.

Logan your atmosphere tingles electric,
dawn light and leaves atremble,
catharsis etching your soul. Against all odds,
hope spreads like truth reflected
in a pond, like two crows making love
in an overhead pine bough, like a bridge
made of rope and slats.

From canyon to canyon we cross
the high suspension, surprised
that our hearts are so loud.

A Collaborative, Commemorative Community Poem compiled from lines and words written by participants of the Logan Poetry Walkabouts of 2018-19, presented at Star's final reading for the Logan City Council on August 20, 2019.

Contributors:
Star Coulbrooke, Alyssa Witbeck Alexander, Brittney Allen, Amy Anderson, Shaun Anderson, Nelda Ault-Dyslin, Shanan Ballam, David Bates, Kendall Becker, Asher Jade Blakely, Sam Capasso, Holly Conger, Jack Daley, Brock Dethier, Terysa Dyer, Carol Foht, Jack Green, Luke Lemmon, Andrew Lonero, Pam Loosle, Elizabeth Lord, Valerie Downes Lusco, Amanda Luzzader, Iris Nielsen, Stephanie Pointer, Nichelle Pomeroy, Kayo Robertson, Paul Rogers, Hilary Shughart, Anne Stark, Adrian Thomson, Aaron Timm, Isaac Timm, Chadd VanZanten

ACKNOWLEDGMENTS

Along with the publication credits and contributors listed at the end of each poem, I extend my grateful acknowledgment to friends, family, and colleagues who have supported me in my poetry career, many of whom I have listed in previous volumes. Special thanks to Jane Catlin whose art graces the covers of my three recent poetry collections and to Robb Kunz who designed this volume. Thanks also to mayors Craig Petersen and Holly Daines, the Logan City Council, and the USU Creative Writing Committee, whose collaboration in founding the poet laureate program has made these poems possible.

www.ingramcontent.com/pod-product-compliance
Lightning Source LLC
Chambersburg PA
CBHW031201090426
42736CB00009B/750